TIME WITH YOU

ANNE-MARIE TUCKER

Illustrations by—Amanda Meador

© 2018 Anne-Marie Tucker

Illustrations and cover design by Amanda Meador. All Rights Reserved. No part of this book may be reproduced in any form or by any electronic or mechanical means, without permission in writing from the author. For permission, write to Tony Meduri TBI Fund Inc. 488 Blagdon CT, Jacksonville, FL 32225, United States

ISBN 978-1-944155-27-8
ISBN 978-1-944155-28-5 ebook

This edition published by Jozef PA of Louisiana LLC under the Jozef Syndicate imprint. For information, write to P.O. Box 318013, Baton Rouge, LA, 70831. Editing by Candace J. Semien. www.jozefsyndicate.com.

Printed in the United States of America

This book is dedicated to my father, my protector, Tony Meduri, who suffered a Traumatic Brain Injury when he was hit by a drugged driver while sitting at a red light in his prized 1934 Ford hotrod.

Tony retired as a police officer after giving 32 years of service to the Delaware Port Authority. Born in Reggio Calabria, Italy and abandoned by his father at two months old, he came to America when he was nine years old with his mother. His life was full of obstacles and challenges, his first was when he broke his neck at age 17.

Paralyzed from the neck down, Tony was told he would never walk again. Proving the doctors wrong, he went through rehabilitation, walked again, and graduated from the police academy.

He became a caregiver for his mother at age 26 when she broke her back and could no longer work. After having three children, he divorced and became a single dad raising his two girls on his own (his son passed at birth).

Tony, my dad, taught me what it means to be strong, to be determined, and to love with all your heart. I became the sole caregiver to him for seven years while raising my own two children and caring for my grandmother until she died in 2014. I learned to love the man after the accident who was no longer the protector, who had no memory and could not do anything for himself. He suffered many years confused, sick, and gradually became wheelchair bound.

I am grateful to have been given another chance to love and care for him.

TABLE OF CONTENTS

II. POEMS

Luv Me With TBI	1
Let's Make New Memories	3
Emotions	4
Restart	5
Tony's Angels	7
TBI	7
Time With You	9
Don't You Remember	12
On the Water	13
Dance With Me	15
Make Moments	18
Calm	19
The Dunes	19
Badge of Courage	21
Put Me First	23

LUV ME WITH TBI
(Traumatic Brain Injury)

It happened when I least expected it
When I wasn't prepared

I didn't see it coming
Now the new me
Struggles to find the words I want to say

I can't focus
My brain lives in a time my luved ones don't

So play pretend with me

I can't do anything for myself
But try to luv the new me
The person whose heart still beats
Who needs your luv

Don't leave me
don't change

Just luv me for who I am now
Luv me with a TBI

LET'S MAKE NEW MEMORIES

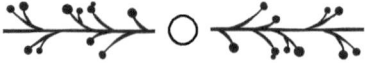

Let's make new memories
Ones as the person I am now...
Someone who struggles to find the words to remember what we used to do
Let's make new memories
To keep me strong and give you hope
One day I might, maybe for a second, remember the old times
But let's make memories for us now
To conquer this obstacle of the new me
The disabled me, the weak me, but the same me

EMOTIONS

This Brain Injury forever changed me
I'm happy, sad, confused
All within minutes
I'm scared
I'm alone in here
I'm not the same but luv me for who I am now
I can't control these emotions
but I always know I will never forget your luv for me

RESTART

Today I am confused, crying and even happy for a few minutes
Even though I am an adult, I sometimes act like a child

You see it's my Brain Injury

I can't control these emotions and I need to restart
I don't know how to ask, so I can only count on the one who
luves me to push the restart button for me

Time for a nap, some new scenery, or just new conversation
I know I look normal and ok but I'm not

Please,
Restart me

TONY'S ANGELS

Are there really such a thing as angels?
Are there actually people who luv me like I am now:
Broken, confused, angry, and aggressive at times
I've even swung at you,
I don't mean it, angel
You see, I just want to go home
I just want to be able to tell you how I'm feeling, angel
Yep you are my angel,
Because even though I've said something or done something to hurt you,
You are still here
You still luv me
See God sent you to me
My angels

TBI
(Traumatic Brain Injury)

To be innocent is what this means to me
To be innocent
Of this accident that I had no control over
Of being mean or cruel
Of not remembering you or times we shared
Of cursing or using foul language to explain how I feel
I am innocent
I have been injured
I can't control it and I'm sorry

TIME WITH YOU

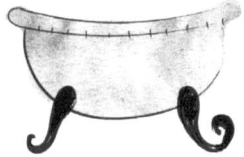

Oh, how I have enjoyed this time with you
Feeding you, bathing you
Laughing with you at those uncontrollable words you use
I still miss my time with you
Even when you didn't know my name
Or recall seeing me that morning
I still miss my time with you

Even though you aren't the same person I knew
I still miss my time with you
Even when you wanted to go home when we were out together
I still miss my time with you
Even when God took you to heaven
I still miss my time with you

DON'T YOU REMEMBER

Don't you remember when you would hold me in your arms,
and tell me you luved me?
Don't you remember when you would ask me if you could go home?
Don't you remember telling me I wasn't your daughter?
I was someone else to you
Don't you remember when you asked me to dance with you?
I joyfully sang and danced with you around your wheelchair
Don't you remember how you used to care for us as children when mom left?

You were there

Don't you remember all those years of caring for us and grandmom?
You never faltered
Don't you remember how you made people smile
Even when you got worse?
Don't you remember buying me that pink lace prom dress that I had to have
when you had no money to spare?
Don't you remember putting on your uniform to work the night shift so you
could see us off to school?
Don't you remember the day you were hit by the drugged driver in your prized
'34 Ford?

The day the man we once knew was gone

I remember
And I still luv you

ON THE WATER

It was your dream to be on the water
To hear the waves crashing in the ocean
Watch the pretty girls on the beach and children play
To feel the sun on your skin
It was your dream to be on the water
So I found a place where you would live the last few years of your life
On the water
When all else failed,
When you were confused, angry
You found peace when you were living on the water
Every day we sat with you on the porch looking out on the water
It calmed you
And the last breath you took,
We made sure that you were still able to hear the crashing of the waves,
At your home on the water

DANCE WITH ME

You told me you wanted to dance
So we played your favorite song
And I sang and danced with you
Around your wheelchair
It's been so long since I've seen your eyes light up like that
It's been so long since I've seen you smile
I actually made you happy
Sometimes I made you sad
So I danced with you
Like we did when I was young
And you would ask me to teach you
But now you taught me that even without the use of your legs
You can dance with me

MAKE MOMENTS

Spending time with me
You will learn to enjoy the moments
Maybe for just a few seconds I'll remember who I used to be
the full, unbroken person
Or maybe I just find comfort in seeing a familiar face,
Because it's that moment that makes me happy,
And I need that moment to make you happy
I need you to turn those moments into long-lasting memories of us together
I don't need a lot of your time,
just that moment
You gave me

We thought we lost you when I got the call saying you were in a coma
being flown to the hospital
You gave me chills
I couldn't breathe
Doc told me when you would awake that you would need 24/7 care
You gave me a second chance
To take care of you like you did me
You had to learn how to eat, walk, and talk all over again
With all the therapy, hospitals, and medicine,
You were never the same
You gave me a chance to teach you and remind you of who you used to be
You taught me how to never give up
You gave me a chance to luv you like my own child,
To care for you
You gave my kids a chance to see what it means to luv,
And care for someone else
After years of suffering, God took you
But you gave me many new memories and more time
You gave me a second chance to know you as more than just my father

CALM

The whispering of the waves calms me
I sometimes can't control what's in my head
But the whispering of the waves calms me
Sometimes I can't find the words to express how I feel
But the whispering of the waves calms me
I know you and luv you but can't recall your name
But the whispering of the waves calms me
When all else fails and I can't get control
The whispering of the waves calms me

THE DUNES

Like me are protectors
Protect our homes and living space from the stormy sea
They can be rebuilt
Like me
They should be respected and maintained
Like me
And even though they can be taken from us and destroyed
They can be rebuilt like me

BADGE OF COURAGE

Where is my badge
I have to go to work
My badge defines me

Now I know who I am
It's a badge of courage

Please take me home
So I can go to work
I can't remember where I left my badge

Help me find the courage
To tell you, dad, that you
Don't work anymore
My hero in uniform
That your life has been taken from you

But you still have your memories and
Your badge of courage

PUT ME FIRST

I saw a butterfly today, he swept by my side
And I felt for the first time
The emptiness is gone

I filled it with memories of you
Images of the full person
Who loved me, whole heartedly
Who always ….
Put me first

Even with so little resources
And many, many obstacles
You always
Put me first

So when you became sick
I gave you many years of love and caregiving
And when you grew tired and weak
God came and took you
So now it's time for me to lose the emptiness

Because I know that you would want me to
Put ME first

A new journey blossoms

www.ingramcontent.com/pod-product-compliance
Lightning Source LLC
Chambersburg PA
CBHW041757040426
42446CB00001B/64